DISCARD

COPYRIGHT @2005

Car Accident Secrets

© 2005 **WWW.CARACCIDENTSECRETS.COM**
DS Publications
Version 1.0.5

COLLECTION MANAGEMENT

05-09	1-2	09-8
1/2012	3- 11	4/2011

Foreword

This reference tool has been written to help consumers know their rights after being involved in a car accident. I have been driving for over 20 years and have been involved in five accidents. Four of the accidents were not my fault at all. Other drivers hit my car. When I was younger I didn't know my rights and gave most of them away just because I didn't have the knowledge of what is contained in this reference tool. After working for several Fortune 500 insurance companies and several claims areas within those companies, I have compiled a reference tool to let the consumer know what to do in case of an auto accident.

The chances of being in an accident today with so many drivers on the road, has increased dramatically. If you do not know your rights you will be giving up valuable amounts of money and benefits you are entitled to as a result of the accident. You probably have been paying your auto insurance since you have been driving which amounts to thousands of dollars. If a bad driver hits you through no fault of yours, then you deserve some compensation.

This book will show you how to protect your rights and obtain compensation for your losses, which include your car repair and any bodily injury and/or pain and suffering. You should follow the instructions in this reference tool if you are ever involved in an accident.

Disclaimer

This book is a reference tool. By purchasing and reading this reference tool, you acknowledge that the author or caraccidentclaims.com will not be liable for your ability or inability to use this book properly. It is up to you on how you handle a claim resulting from an accident. This book was written to provide information only on how to file an accident claim. It is intended to help you understand the process of filing an accident claim and receiving a settlement. It is not intended to provide legal advice. Recommendations are made without any guarantee and the author/publisher/caraccidentsecrets.com disclaims all liability incurred in connection with the use of this information.

If you are unsure of how to proceed with an auto claim resulting from an accident consult with an attorney that deals with auto accidents.

Table of Contents

Chapter

1

Reviewing your Current Insurance Policy Coverage

Checking your current coverage is the first step

T he coverage that you have on your policy is one of the most important steps prior to ever having an accident. Having the correct insurance will protect you in case the other driver does not have insurance and you have to use your policy to pay for your damages and injuries.

The key points to review in your policy are:

- Policy limits and deductibles

- Towing , Rental vehicles

- Windshield coverage

A. ICON KEY

📁 Valuable information

✏️ Test your knowledge

✋ Important Notes

You should have a declaration page from your insurance company that shows the information above. Make sure the information is what you specified to your agent. If not contact your agent immediately and request a change.

There are six types of basic insurance. They may be called other terms from what is listed below but these 6 cover the most widely used terms. These types may vary between states and certain states requirements may be different or not offered. Check with your insurance agent if you have questions.

Reviewing
Insurance limits are important. You should have enough coverage to protect your family and home in case of an accident. Insurance companies sell umbrella policies which can protect you to 1 million dollars. Check with your agent & review your policy.

6 Basic types of Insurance

I. Bodily Injury Liability : This pays your legal defense costs and claims against you if your vehicle injures or takes someone's life. Covers family members living with you and others driving with your permission.

II. Property Damage Liability : This pays your legal defense costs and claims against you if your vehicle damage's someone else's property. This does not cover your property or vehicle.

III. Medical Payments : This coverage pays medical expenses resulting from an accident for you and anyone in the vehicle at the time of the accident. This also pays for you or family member who are injured while riding in someone else's vehicle or as a pedestrian walking.

IV. Collision : This coverage pays for repairs to your vehicle caused by a collision with another vehicle or object, regardless of who is responsible.

V. Comprehensive Physical Damage : This coverage will pay for damage to your vehicle that are from theft, fire, vandalism, nature (ie:hail) or unintended damage like a rock hitting your windshield. Some insurance companies have separated windshield coverage since windshields being cracked with rocks is such a common occurrence. Make sure your coverage is adequate)

VI. Uninsured/Underinsured Driver : This coverage will pay for costs related to damage to your vehicle and injuries for you and any family members/guests in your vehicle cause by an uninsured driver. This will also cover underinsured drivers, these are drivers who did not have enough coverage on their insurance policy.

2 Mandatory types of Insurance

There are 2 types of insurance that are mandatory in many states, Personal Injury and Uninsurance.

I. Personal Injury : This coverage is what is referred to as No-Fault. This means that no matter who caused the accident, if a person is injured and missing employment due to the injuries that they have the right to collect an amount of what is necessary and reasonable for medical expenses and between 75% and 100% of wages that are lost due to missing employment.

II.   Uninsurance : This coverage handles the following

   a. Unregistered/Uninsured Vehicle - If the vehicle that hit the injured persons vehicle is not insured, the injured person has to go against his/her own policy for compensation

   b. Hit and Run - This occurs when one vehicle hits another and then leaves the scene of the accident. And no one can identify the car that left the scene.

c. Force - Your vehicle has been forced off the road with no physical contact with another vehicle. If the unknown vehicle forced off the road hits a tree, pole, another car etc. the injured person would have an uninsured claim against his/her own policy.

Personal Injury - No Fault Information
Agents offer a deductible on no fault to save you money on your yearly premium. You should have sufficient coverage because the injured party pays for expenses out of their own pocket. If you were at fault you could be liable for EACH person's deductible.

Insurance Problem
Many people purchase the 20K/40K policy which saves them money on the yearly premium. It is recommended that you have at least 50K/100K or an umbrella policy.

An umbrella policy helps add a layer of protection over and above your auto and homeowners insurance policies. If a claim against either of these policies exceeds your coverage limits, an umbrella policy would help cover the outstanding obligation

Test

1) What does Comprehensive Physical Damage cover ?

2) What percentage of lost wages should you be able to recover if you are injured from an accident?

This page left intentionally blank

Accidents & Lawyers

Some background about car accidents

I f you are involved in a car accident it could be major or minor. I have been in several but nothing major (no broken bones or serious injuries). If you are in a serious accident where you have broken bones or worse like someone is fatally injured, it is recommended you seek legal counsel.

Some types of car accidents – The 3 M's:

- Major - Serious or Fatal accidents where car is totaled and/or injuries are serious or life threatening

- Medium accidents where you may have muscle tears, skin abrasions, bruises and/or serious car damage.

- Minor accidents (ie: fender bender) where you may have minor neck/back, minor car damage (ie: cracked windshield or bumper, scratches on your vehicle)

I have been involved in a medium and minor accident where I successfully received compensation for both accidents without using a lawyer. I will go over my steps which I used in each case later in this book.

The benefits of dealing with the insurance company without a lawyer are:

1) Lawyers typically take 1/3 of the final settlement which could add up to a lot especially if you are going for a small settlement.

2) You get the money faster. Insurance companies typically want to settle the claim as fast as possible and close the claim.

The con of dealing without a lawyer is:

1) You may not get all the compensation you are entitled to.

This page left intentionally blank

Chapter
3

What to do at the Accident Scene

Steps to help you through gathering information

These steps are listed in the back of the book on an easy checklist that should be kept in your car with your insurance card.

1 **Check everyone** - When an accident occurs the first thing you should do is make sure everyone is ok and does not need medical attention. Some states require by law, that you must seek medical attention for injured parties or you could possibly face criminal charges or a civil lawsuit.

If someone needs medical attention try and get a person not involved in the accident to phone police or an ambulance. No one should leave the scene of the accident. If the accident is minor, the police may not respond. The police will usually respond to accidents that involve injury, fatality, no insurance, or other driving offences, hit and run or if a fight breaks out over who is at fault.

One of my concerns after my minor accident was that I didn't call the police. I found out from the insurance company that it is not required when there is minor damage and no major injuries.

2 **Look for witnesses** - If someone does phone the police for you make sure you ask them if they saw the accident. If they did get their name and address before they leave the scene.

3 **Protect the area** - Turn on your hazard lights and if possible raise the hood of your car to alert other drivers there is a problem. If it is night use flares and reflectors to alert traffic to the situation.

4 **Take pictures** - Many people now have cell phones with built in cameras so before any cars move after the collision, take a few pictures. If you don't have a cell phone with a camera buy a disposable camera and keep it in your glove compartment.

5 **Do not Argue but Speak Up** - Don't argue with the other driver or passengers about who is at fault. If police do arrive to take a police report definitely speak up and do not let the other driver be the only one giving his/her version of what happened.

6 **Get Information** - The most important step after an accident is to get the other drivers information. After both my accidents the first thing I did was get the other drivers plate number (memorize it if possible) in case they drove away. But the biggest piece of information you need is contained on one document **THE OTHER DRIVERS INSURANCE CARD.** This contains Name/Address/VIN/Name of their insurance company.

7 **Do not Sign Anything** - Do not sign any paper that shows you are responsible for the accident. Keep your notes and comments to yourself. Admit nothing and sign nothing even if you think you caused the accident.

If you sign something that releases the other party from responsibility your insurance company's rights will be jeopardized and your insurance company may refuse to pay for damage to your vehicle.

8 **Do not Accept Payment** - Even if the accident is minor you should not accept payment at the scene. There could be hidden damage to your vehicle or you may have minor whiplash/back pain which will not show up until later.

If the other driver doesn't want the accident reported to his insurance company, he can work that out with your insurance company after all costs are known. But in the end it is up to you (the injured party) to decide if you should collect from your insurance company or theirs. I have my own opinion on this which I will discuss later in the book.

Test

3) What are the 2 most important things that are needed after an accident?

4) Why should you not accept money at the scene of the accident?

Chapter

4

Medical Attention

More information about #1-Checking everyone's condition at the scene

After an accident your body is full of adrenaline. Adrenaline protects the body and blocks any pain when there is a sudden shock or event. You will not be fully aware of your injuries until about half hour or more after the accident.

If you haven't been taken by an ambulance to a hospital but you have any severe pain after the accident, get to a doctor immediately. If you were thrown against your seatbelt, became unconscious or were struck by the air bag deploying you should seek an immediate medical attention.

Seat belts have caused numerous deaths from internal injuries. The sudden whip action of being thrown forward in the seat by a violent stop has been known to cause the spleen to rupture and start to bleed. Some people have been sent home from hospitals or medical centers without proper treatment only to die of undiagnosed internal bleeding.

My medium accident injury did not appear till morning. I had severe back pain and so did my passenger. The next day we went to a Sports Medicine Center for x-rays on our necks and spine. Do not worry about the cost for this as you should be reimbursed by the insurance company.

Follow up any emergency hospital visit with your family doctor. Your doctor will make a determination on when you can return to work, any therapy treatments you may need and work with the insurance company. Your doctor will also handle the claim forms for the medical insurance coverage. The claims and any prescriptions, muscle relaxants etc may be reimbursed.

This page left intentionally blank

Chapter 5

Witnesses/Photos

More information about Witnesses, Accident Area, Pictures

I t is important to get the names of witnesses after you make sure everyone is ok and medical attention is not needed. In both of my accidents no witnesses were around. My passenger was the only other witness but she was also injured.

In most accidents you will have witnesses but they will not wait since they are probably driving somewhere too. If there are bystanders, ask if they saw the accident. If they did, write down their name/address and phone number.

Make sure to get the drivers information, preferably off their insurance card. Also get the names/addresses of the passengers, if there are any. If the insurance card is not available use their drivers license and also take down their driver's license number. Make sure to get the plate number of the vehicle.

Photographs are also a valuable tool to help show the conditions of the road and the surrounding environment. You should take pictures of :

✓ Any skid marks

✓ The cars before they are moved, if possible

✓ Surroundings, stop signs/lights etc.

✓ The damage on each vehicle

Photographs can help you back up your statements in a police report. Sometimes the officer who comes to the scene does not get all the information correctly which happened in my case. The insurance companies rely on the police report to determine who is at fault. Photos may also help you with details that you did not notice at the time of the accident.(hidden stop sign, posted speed limit etc.).

The insurance company will also use the photos to back up your claim. Get the photos developed as soon as possible, ideally with a date on the back.

In the case of severe accidents where you may be hospitalized, you will have to rely on the police report. The report will list witnesses that you can follow up with after you are well. If the report just contains the names of the witnesses, you can call them and ask if they could mail you a statement of what they saw at the accident scene.

Since many cell phones now have built in cameras, they are the perfect tool to use to record the accident. If you do not have one of these it is recommended you keep a disposable camera in your glove compartment. They cost under 5$ and will have a sufficient amount of photos that you can take of the accident scene.

Chapter

Information

More information about Getting information

Th{here} is an accident form at the back of the book that will help you keep track of all the information being presented here. It can also aid you if you need to file a police report.

Depending upon the damage from the accident and the insurance company, you may or may not need to file a police report. For my minor accident I didn't file a police report. For my medium accident the police came to the scene and filed a police report taking both drivers statements.

The insurance card and driver's license are your two most important pieces of information that you need to get at the accident scene. Write down as much information as you can from both pieces. Also check the driver's license for any restrictions (ie: glasses required to drive). The restrictions will show up as a number typed on the face of the license with an explanation on the back.

Write down your statement of the accident and write the street names/intersection of where it occurred, the time of day, weather conditions and any passengers.

If your car needs to be towed, make sure you get it towed to WHERE you want. Do not be rushed or pushed into something by the tow truck driver. The safest place is your dealer or a dealer for your make of car. If possible have the dealer tow your car.

and protect your rights.

If the police come to the scene and issue a warning or ticket to the other driver, this is very important information that your insurance company will need to know. If you know the other driver is 100% at fault make sure you inquire with the police about issuing the other driver a ticket or warning. Do not be afraid to speak up

This page left intentionally blank

Chapter

7

What to do After the Accident

The scene has been cleared information taken, now what ?

k, You are now either home or you are continuing your trip or hospitalized. If the accident was minor or medium the next step is your choice. You can either file a claim yourself or get a lawyer.

Do I Need a Lawyer?

IF THE ACCIDENT WAS MAJOR - SEVERE (see pg 4), IT IS RECOMMEDED YOU GET A LAWYER IMMEDIATELY ONCE YOU ARE ABLE TO. You can find lawyers who will take pro-bono (no money upfront) cases in the yellow pages.

For minor/medium accidents, if it is not your fault and you want to handle the claim yourself, it is your right to do so. This book will guide you in getting the most for your claim without using an attorney.

If the accident was your fault, you can let your insurance company handle the entire claim. Ask your insurance company if you need a lawyer.

If the accident was 100% the other drivers fault then you can file a claim against the other driver's insurance company and handle the claim yourself. Even if the accident was shared (ie: you both ran a stop sign) you can still handle your own claims.

Some examples where the other driver is 100% at fault:

✓ Front end collision at stop sign

✓ You were rear ended

✓ Other driver runs a red light or stop sign

Most lawyers make you think settling a car accident claim is difficult when in fact it is relatively quite simple. Most claims involve no more than calling the adjuster and keeping track of your receipts.

You can handle the claim best by yourself because

✓ You know what happened better than anyone else

✓ You know what injuries you have and what physical condition you are in

You must however do things in a timely fashion. Do not wait to file the claim or report the accident.

If you are still unsure about handling the claim on your own: In some states lawyers will give you a free consultation to discuss your claim, others may charge a nominal fee. Even if you pay a few hundred dollars for a consultation you will come out way ahead of the person who hires an attorney to take on the case. If you speak with a lawyer be honest and describe the accident. Tell him you would like to handle the claim on your own and need to know what to do to file successfully. You could also tell the lawyer that if you feel the case is too much to handle after you start it or if you need to sue, that you will bring the records back to them to handle the case. Make sure you write down the information the lawyer gives you.

Failure to find out the laws as they pertain to you in your state and to act on those laws accordingly may severely affect your claim.

Lawyers will try and get you the most money from a claim however they want a piece of your claim. You might find the lawyer trying to make you sign papers to handle your claim after the initial consultation. DO NOT let the lawyer intimidate you into signing papers to handle your claim. Just tell them you need time to decide. You can talk to any number of lawyers until you find one you like.

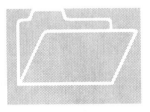

Except in complicated cases, a lawyer will usually get 10% - 25% above what you can get yourself once you understand the process. Plus it will take a lot longer. Insurance companies want to close cases as soon as possible. And the lawyer will take 24% - 40% of your compensation as a fee.

In some cases, you will need the skills of an experienced lawyer. You injuries may be serious and the compensation amount varies greatly. Or the other drivers insurance company refuses to settle with you in good faith.

There are no set in stone rules about whether you need to hire a lawyer. The decision has to do with how you feel the claim is going when you attempt to settle on your own. Is the insurance company cooperating with you? Are they not responding to your calls?

You may just feel overwhelmed, or have to deal with an adjuster who refuses to honor your car damage repair estimates saying you were more at fault than the other driver. Or maybe after you present your claims, dollar amounts and the insurance company only offers half of your expenses. In these cases you should consult an attorney.

If you have been keeping good records it will be a great help if you ever need to speak to an attorney down the road.

There are some claims which certainly require a lawyer consultation. Some examples are:

- ✓ If the accident resulted in injuries that significantly affect your physical capabilities

- ✓ If you appearance is marred for a long time or even permanently

- ✓ Or if you have a history of neck and back problems that might reduce your claim

- ✓ Broken bones

- ✓ Fatalities

Figuring out how much serious injuries are worth may require a lawyer. The amount of compensation is determined by how severe the injuries were and the amount that other claimants have received for similar situations.

The severity of injuries is measured by the following:

- ✓ Amount of medical bills

- ✓ Type of injury

- ✓ Length of time it takes to recover

Once the amount of your compensation gets to a high level it may be worth the expense to have a lawyer handle the claim to ensure you get the most compensation.

However most claims filed do not fall into this category so you should plan on attempting to handle the claim on your own. It requires a little work but not much more than if you use a lawyer. Even if you use a lawyer you still have to follow the same steps of gathering information. And you can always hire a lawyer later if it becomes necessary, but you cannot get rid of a lawyer without paying him some of your settlement. Even if you are not happy with the amount he settles your case for, you still may be liable to pay his/her bill. Then you will have to negotiate on your own or hire another lawyer.

If you hire a lawyer he will tell you not to talk with the adjuster anymore. The adjuster will have to deal directly with the lawyer. The lawyer will then have to call you with questions and get back to the adjuster with the answers. You will also have to sign forms that the medical and wage information will go to him first which he will evaluate for errors.

If your claim is straightforward you will not have any problem with the medical reports. When you go to see a doctor let him know your injury is from an auto accident. They will fill the forms out so the insurance companies can understand the exact problems.

If you decide not to hire a lawyer you should still document and save everything related to the accident. All correspondence, letters, receipts etc. If for some reason you need a lawyer later, everything will be of value. A diary is especially important and is discussed in the next chapter. Keeping a diary lets you remember the extent of the pain, if you don't keep track you may forget. I kept diaries for both my accidents. When I look back at my medium accident I can't believe how much pain and inconvenience the accident was.

When the time comes to settle the claim you will be advised by your lawyer, if you retained one. He will contact the insurance company adjuster and negotiate a settlement for pain and suffering. Then he will ask for your approval of the offer. If you approve the check it will be sent to the lawyer. He will take his percentage and send the balance to you.

If you are without a lawyer, the adjuster will negotiate with you and send the check directly to you after an agreement. See the Finalizing Claim chapter.

How well you settle your claim depends on how well you start it and keep it going. The sooner you get organized and begin documenting the better.

You should have:

- A folder for all your paperwork specific for the accident

- Accident report

- Claim number from your company

- Claim number from the other insurance company

- Diary

- All Receipts (doctors, store, etc)

On the next page is a chart showing different accident conditions

Comparison Chart

Type of accident	Fault	File against which insurance co?	Handle yourself ?
A. MAJOR	YOURS or SHARED		GET LAWYER
B. MAJOR	OTHER DRIVER or not known		GET LAWYER
C. MEDIUM	100% YOURS	YOURS	YES OR LET YOUR INSURANCE HANDLE
D. MEDIUM	50% or some shared % amount EACH DRIVER	OTHER DRIVERS	YES
E. MEDIUM	100% OTHER DRIVER	OTHER DRIVERS	YES
F. MINOR	100% YOURS	YOURS	YES OR LET YOUR INSURANCE HANDLE
G. MINOR	100% OTHER DRIVER	OTHER DRIVERS	YES
H. MINOR	50% or some shared % amount EACH DRIVER	OTHER DRIVERS	YES

Handling the Claim on your Own

1. Determine Fault

Fault in an accident is very important to the insurance claim. That is why it is important to speak up when the police come to the scene. The insurance companies will determine payout based on the percentage of who is at fault. The police report will also show who is at fault per the police officer's conclusion.

2. File a Police Report

Normally if there is more than $1,000 in damage or injuries, a police report needs to be filed, if the police did not come to the scene. You will have to go to the police station nearest to where the accident occurred to file the report.

The accident report must be filed in person, so you must go to the station in that area. You cannot phone in an accident report.

Before you go down to make your report, take time to write down your statement of what happened as you remember it if you have already not done that. When it is complete take the accident form in the back of this book and your statement to the police station to file.

If the police did show up at the scene a report should be ready within a week (depending on the size of the city). You can request a copy usually for around $10. A copy of the report will get your claim moving faster. Save the receipt since this is also another charge that will be paid by the insurance company.

3. Contact YOUR Insurance Company

Contact your insurance company as soon as you are able to report the accident. Give the claim representative all of the information you collected from the accident scene. They will also ask if there were any injuries. Tell the agent that you are not sure (some injuries may not have appeared) and may be having a doctor take a look for possible injuries, if you have already gone to the doctor let them know. The claim representative will also ask if you were wearing your seatbelt. The answer should always be YES. Once they have entered all the information they will give you a claim number. Write it down and keep everything in a folder for easy access.

Tell the claims representative that you are filing your report at your insurance company "FOR RECORD ONLY". This lets the representative know that you will be filing a claim against the OTHER DRIVER'S insurance policy.

your money.

If you will be looking for a settlement without a lawyer (D, E, G, H from chart on previous page), TELL YOUR INSURANCE COMPANY YOU WILL BE FILING A CLAIM AGAINST THE OTHER DRIVERS INSURANCE POLICY. If you do it that way you will not have to wait for your insurance company to handle the process, which is slow and may not give you the most for

4. Contact THE OTHER DRIVERS Insurance Company

Contact the other driver's insurance company. Tell them in this order:

- ✓ You were involved in an accident with one of their policyholders

- ✓ Ask if the accident was reported by the policyholder.

- ✓ Tell them you are filing a claim AGAINST THEIR POLICY

The other insurance company will ask the same questions you just gave to your insurance company. **When they ask how you feel: Tell them where you are having pain if you are, NEVER say you are good/fine or you don't have any initial pain/problems. Just say you aren't sure and you may be going to your doctor.**

If you are going to consult a lawyer you should just tell the claim representative at the opening of the call.

Rental Car

If your car was damaged and had to be towed (Medium accident) tell the other drivers insurance company that you need a rental car. Find one in your yellow pages before you call and get prices on an equivalent car. You are by law required to get a car that compares with the type you currently drive. In most cases the other driver's insurance company will call the rental place you have in mind and handle the entire transaction. If you can't reach the other drivers insurance company and still need a rental car immediately (like weekends), just tell the rental agency that this is for an auto insurance claim. You may have to pay up front so save all the receipts and paperwork.

You will get the rental car for the entire time it takes to repair your car. The insurance companies will usually set a standard time (10 days) but if your car takes longer don't worry, the insurance company will extend the time if you contact them once you have heard from your car repair site.

If you don't need a rental car or your car was in a minor accident but your car is still drivable, YOU ARE ENTITLED TO LOSS OF USE dollars ONCE YOUR CAR GOES IN FOR REPAIR.

Fixing your Car

After you have discussed a rental car (if needed), talk to the claim representative about an adjuster going to see your car. Also let the claim representative know if there was any towing fees (you will be reimbursed for those so save your receipts)

Most companies today send adjusters out to your car to review the damage. If the car is not drivable (ie: at the repair shop), tell the claim representative the cars location. YOU HAVE THE RIGHT TO HAVE YOUR CAR FIXED WHERE YOU WANT. I used my dealer in my medium accident case. They had done work for me in the past and I trusted them.

If you are still driving the car have the adjuster come to YOUR place of work or your home. You are not required to take it to ONE OF THEIR centers.

Do not let an adjuster do anything to the damage like trying to pop out a dent. I had an adjuster take out a piece of sandpaper and try to sandpaper a damaged spot. Needless to say he didn't come close to touching my car and I reported him to my company. He tried that move so I wouldn't just keep the money and not have the repair done.

Adjusters today also have the ability today to issue checks on the spot. But if you cash a check then that is the most you will ever get for your property damage. Also make sure the check says for PROPERTY DAMAGE ONLY. If it doesn't DO NOT CASH IT and ask them to issue you a new check with the correct wording. The reason you should not cash it is because you may have medical expenses and some companies try to get away with having one check cover all without you knowing.

So before an adjuster comes out to look at your car you should get quotes (at least 2) for the damage. YOU ARE ENTITLED TO THE REPLACEMENT OF ORIGINAL MANUFACTURED PARTS not generic or no name brand part. THEY SHOULD BE THE ORIGINAL OEM REPLACEMENT PARTS. Make sure when you get estimates that you specify you want quotes on OEM parts.

Injuries

Most likely you will have some form of an injury, like neck or back pain. The claim representative will open a separate claim for each person involved. And it will also be a different claim number than the one for your vehicle damage. This is the INJURED PARTY CLAIM. Make sure you let the claim representative know that you want to open a separate injury claim.

Each injury claim will be judged and a final amount determined on its own merits. This means your claim may be finalized before any of your injured party claims depending on the extent of injuries.

You may be asked to sign papers to release information concerning your medical history and wage earnings. For my minor accident I just faxed a copy of my paycheck to determine the hourly rate for the time I missed work going to the doctors.

Types of Injuries

Soft Injuries:

Injuries such as sprained or strained back, neck, knee or ankle are referred to as soft tissue injuries because they involve only muscles and other soft tissue. Insurance companies regard them as less serious and usually assign a lower multiplier. Insurers reason that soft tissue injuries are usually not permanent or dangerous regardless of how painful they may be. And insurance companies also know that, should a claim ever get to court, it would be difficult for an injured person to prove clearly what the soft tissue injuries were.

Back or Joint Injuries:

Generally, if you have a narrowing, displacement or other damage to a vertebra, an injury to a disc in the spine, or a dislocation, ligament or cartilage injury to any joint, you will most likely suffer some permanent effect, even if only slight. The pain may subside and the injury stabilize but there is a medical likelihood that some pain, discomfort or lack of mobility will continue or will reoccur as you get older.

If you have such an injury, part of your claim for damages should be for permanent injury and therefore higher compensation. And if you can get your doctor to mention in your medical records the possibility of some permanent or residual effect, you will have documented support for your claim. The simplest way to get your doctor to make a notation about permanent effects is to ask.

Towards the last part of your treatment, ask your doctor's opinion about whether there is a possibility that you may have recurring or degenerative problems as a result of your injuries. If the answer is yes, ask that the doctor note it in your medical records. Even if the doctor does not note the possibility of permanent problems, you can still raise the possibility in your claim.

Chapter

8

Keep a Diary

One of the most important things you should do

I f you hired an attorney they would tell you to keep a diary. This is very important especially if you are handling your own claim without an attorney. In both my accidents I kept a diary and it pays off literally when you go to settle the claim.

Neither of my cases went to trial since the insurance companies are looking to settle as fast as they can and close the case. They also do not want to pay court fees to have a trial and that is another reason to handle a claim on your own. The insurance company is more likely to give you a high settlement value just to save them the hassles of court.

If on the rare chance it goes to trial, the insurance company may ask you questions under oath, a procedure called Examination for Discovery. You are questioned so they can discover the strength and weaknesses of your case. They want to know how it will impress a judge if your case does go to court. The courts compensate a persons pain and suffering by comparing the case to other previous cases. When you keep a written diary it will be a lot easier for you under examination, all you have to do is refer to the diary. With everything written day by day you can show how your recovery progressed. I kept my diary in electronic form on computer which made it even easier.

In the first few days make notes on your pain, discomfort, anxiety and loss of sleep which all adds to your compensation. This will also help if you need to report aches/pains to your doctor.

The average claim takes six months to settle. My medium accident took 2 months to settle, my minor accident took 3 weeks to settle. Again this will all vary on the accident and the other driver's insurance company you are dealing with.

What should you Record in the Diary?

Start with the day and time and then list

1) Part of your body that is causing you pain (from most to least painful)

2) Description of pain - include the severity, the type of pain and the length of pain.

To describe the severity use words like:

a. Mild

b. Moderate

c. Moderately Severe

d. Severe

e. Excruciating

To describe the type of pain use words like:

a. Sharp

b. Twinges

c. Aching

d. Discomfort

e. Soreness

f. Shooting Pain

g. Spasm

h. Numbness

i. Tingling

j. Stiffness

k. Annoying

l.   Gnawing

m.   Stabbing

n.   Radiating

o.   Irritating.

3)   What brought on the pain - did you engage in any activities that triggered or aggravated the pain?

4)   Medication and Treatment - What types of medicine? What dosage? Did you get treatment (Physical Therapy)

5)   Activities - Did you have problems performing any activities? Did you suffer afterwards?

6)   Loss of work hours including overtime/job opportunities - make sure you document

7)   Special events/Vacations - If you missed any special events due to the accident document that. I missed a 40th birthday party the day of my accident and kept the invitation in my diary to show proof.

You may be entitles to compensation for family, educational or other losses. You will need good documentation. You should start your diary immediately after the accident.

Physical and Emotional Distress:

It is not only pain that gives you a right to be compensated, but also any other kind of physical discomfort. Loss of sleep, trouble eating or digesting, stomach upset and the side effects of medication are just some of the physical miseries in addition to pain for which you have a right to be compensated.

Emotional difficulties, too, can be compensated. Physical injuries can cause stress, embarrassment, depression or strains on family relationships. Examples are, the inability to take care of children, anxiety over the effects to an unborn child or interference to sexual relations.

As with pain, however, this other physical or emotional suffering can be difficult to demonstrate. An effective way to show you've suffered physical discomfort is to report it to your doctor, who will note it in your medical file. As stated before, insurance adjusters more readily accept as true something that appears in a medical record than something that you report directly to the adjuster.

If your discomfort or emotional distress is serious enough that you have to seek assistance from someone other that the doctor treating your original injury, these costs also become part of your medical expenses. Be sure to see your own doctor for a referral and then the problem will also be recorded in your medical records. The records of the person assisting you can serve as proof of the problem. Therefore, when it comes time to finalize your claim, do not forget to get a copy of these medical records as well.

Life Disruptions:

Accident injuries can cause a number of unfortunate results that cannot easily be assigned dollar values but which amount to very real and considerable losses. And since money is the only way these losses can be compensated, they must be figured into your damages compensation.

There is no restriction on the types of non-monetary losses that can increase your general damages. Anything important to you that you missed because of your injuries can be included in a claim for compensation. Here are some of the more common kinds of non-monetary losses for which compensation is paid.

Missed Vacation or Recreation:

If your injuries have caused you to cancel a vacation, family visit or other trip or event, you are entitled to extra compensation because of it. Similarly, if you have had to give up your regular recreation activities for an extended time you are entitled to compensation for that loss.

Cancelled Special Event:

If your injuries made it impossible for you to attend an important or personally meaningful event such as a wedding, funeral, graduation, conference or reunion, you are entitled to compensation for the loss. In order for an adjuster to take your claim for compensation seriously, it must be a one-time event that will not be repeated.

Besides reporting injuries in your diary and to your doctor, take photographs of the injuries. If you are in a cast, have cuts scrapes etc.. then take some pictures. By the time your case settles your wounds may heal and pictures can show more information to an insurance company.

Here is a sample Diary entry:

July 6th 2004 :

2:00am: Woke up in extreme pain. Shooting pain in back and neck moderate to severe. Took 2 advils and used Flexall muscle relaxer on back. Couldn't get back to sleep until 5am.

7:00am: Still in extreme pain. Shooting pain in back and neck moderate to severe . Took 2 more advils and phoned doctors office.

10:00am: Went to doctors for X-ray on back and neck 125.00$ charge. Gave prescription for Coedine 50mg. Filled prescription cost 60$. Doctor also recommended physical therapy.

This page left intentionally blank

Chapter

9

On the Road to Getting Better

Continue gaining your health and activities back

A lot of injuries in minor and medium accidents will result in soft tissue damage to the neck. In fact, over 65% are reported with most claims. The neck takes the most force in a car accident.

Because your seat belt holds your upper body back to the seat and doesn't allow major movement of the torso, and the lower part of the body is already in a sitting position, the head and neck are the most exposed for whiplash type injuries. The majority of these injuries (soft tissue) recover within 30 days. About 30% with these type of injuries will suffer longer than one month.

Early intervention and active treatment is effective for rehabilitation, passive treatment is not as effective. Allowing an injured party to remain inactive will seriously delay their recovery. Some insurance accident benefits are provided to help the immediate needs of accident victims. Whether you are a driver, passenger or even a pedestrian, you may receive accident benefits if you are involved in an auto accident. These benefits are paid regardless of who was at fault in the accident, either you or the other driver. These benefits will be given in the form of an advance which goes against your claim. You can also get advances against your lost wages in order to pay for necessities such as food, rent, utility bills etc.

Depending on the insurance coverage you have these benefits could also include payment of your medical and hospital bills that are not covered by any other plan. Also after a waiting period (which varies by State) the insurance company may also provide a weekly disability benefit if you are prevented from returning to work due to your injuries. The adjuster can explain the details that apply to your claim.

This page left intentionally blank

Settling Your Claim

Your record keeping will finally pay off

N ow that you are feeling better , the rental car returned, your car damage repaired and back at home, it may be time to settle. Make sure your health has returned as much as possible. Your diary entries should be small or non existent at this point.

In most cases an insurance company must compensate the injured party for the following:

✓ Medical care and related expenses

✓ Lost Income - whether full-time, part-time or self employed

✓ Pain and Suffering

✓ Permanent physical disability or disfigurement

✓ Loss of social and/or educational experiences including special events, training, vacation, recreation

✓ Emotional damages such as depression, strain on family relationships, stress, the inability to take care of children, anxiety over not being at work or interference with sexual relations

While the way each insurance company calculates the amount differs, it probably will be one of two main ways. The first is to use an amount given to previous claimants for similar accidents. The second is a formula to calculate the amount.

The formula is described on the next page.

The Secret Formula

It's simple to calculate the amount of money that has been spent during an accident or wages that are lost from a job. However there is not an easy way to put a figure on pain and suffering, missed recreation or missed special activities. I missed a 40th birthday party. That party will never happen again for that person. What kind of value should be put on that special occasion? Well, the insurance company has a formula that will apply additional compensation for such situations.

At the beginning of the negotiations on a claim the adjuster will add up all the medical expenses related to the injury. This will become the base figure the adjuster uses to figure out the final amount and determines how much to award for pain, suffering and other non monetary loss.

The adjuster will multiply the base amount by 1.5 or 2 when the injuries are minor and up to 5 when the injuries are serious or long lasting. In a major serious accident the multiplier might even be higher depending on the conditions but those cases should be handled by a lawyer.

So the formula is as follows

TOTAL MEDICAL COSTS x multiplier (1.5 -5) + LOST INCOME

This is ONLY the starting point for negotiations.

Several things determine how large a multiplier to use on your claim. They are listed below:

✓ Pain of Injury

✓ Length and invasiveness of the medical treatment for your injuries

✓ How obvious the medical evidence of the injury was

✓ The visibility and severity of any permanent effects of your injury

✓ The length of time it took you to recover

The multiplier also depends on the type of medical treatment given. Hospital treatment for injuries is given more weight than physical therapy, chiropractic therapy, massage therapy and acupuncture.

Once you know how the insurance companies use the formula to start the negotiations with you, you are more halfway to figuring out the total value of your claim for injuries.

Another factor in deciding how much your claim is worth is how the insurance company feels a jury would decide on your claim if the claim ended up in a court of law. The insurance company must also include the cost of a legal battle as well as what the jury might award you. This would include hiring attorneys, court appearances, filing motion fees etc.

When you add all those costs it is easy to see why the insurance company would rather settle out of court and without lawyers involved.

Another piece to the formula is the extent to which each person is at fault for the accident. This will also determine how much an insurance company will settle a claim for. The formula on the previous page will tell you how much the injuries would be worth but then you need to figure in the at fault percentage to get a final starting value.

So the final formula is as follows

((TOTAL MEDICAL COSTS x multiplier (1.5 -5) + LOST INCOME) * (AT FAULT %))

Substituting some real world value's :

Total Medical Costs - 1100, Multiplier of 3, No lost Income and other driver was 100% at fault

$((1,100 * 3 + 0) * (1.00)) = 3,300$ For 50% at fault $((1,100 * 3 + 0) * (.50)) = 1,650$

If your accident was completely someone else's fault (like you were rear ended) then you would receive the full 100%. If you were mostly at fault then the value of your claim may be greatly reduced. More than likely you will get a small amount which the insurance company refers to as a "nuisance value".

Maximize your Settlement

The following items will help you maximize your settlement amount. They are another important part to settling your accident claim.

DOCUMENTATION

This can't be stressed enough. You must keep good records of the accident and your expenses. Be organized and neat, keep your documentation in an easily accessible folder. Write everything down that you think is important to the accident claim. Also keep track of the date/time/name of the adjusters that you contact and that contact you. Your diary should be updated daily if possible.

PATIENCE

The longer the recovery takes the higher the compensation will be. This does not mean that you can unnecessarily postpone filing the final claim information which would be fraud. Fraud is punishable by law so DO NOT create any fraudulent claims. When you are feeling better, that's when you should file your documentation to the insurance company. You are entitled by law to be fully recovered from your injuries or recovered as fully as possible.

An insurance company will usually advance 75% of lost wages if you were not at fault in the accident. If you have some fault in the accident they may cut that figure down accordingly. In some cases they may advance more but not all of your wage entitlement. The insurance companies hold back some of your wages to put pressure on you to settle early. Don't worry, you are entitle to 75-100% of your lost wages (based on fault again). The pain and suffering part is the negotiable part.

JUMPING TOO SOON

An insurance company may even try to settle with you early with a low initial offer. If you have been out of work, the adjuster knows it and figures you need the money to pay your bills. So a lot of people jump at the first offer because they need the cash. DO NOT do this, even when you are negotiating your final amount with the insurance company. Even for the final settlement, the insurance company will low-ball you with a figure just to see if you will take it. Make sure you have some amounts in mind (use a few different multipliers) from the formula in front of you when you are on the phone with the adjuster discussing the final amount. In my minor case the insurance company started at 200$. My range was 150 - 375. So I told him 200 was too low and he jumped right to 500$. His mistake! I looked at my paper and immediately said yes that was a fair offer. (still not sounding happy). He jumped too high too soon. If he had went to 350$, I would have taken it but he went higher than my range so of course I took it.

The Check

Make sure you are fully recovered before you tell the adjuster you are ready to settle the claim. Once you sign the release form and get the final check that's it. You cannot go back to the insurance company later and claim you have additional pain or the pain has come back. The release form releases the insurance company from any further liability in your claim relating to that accident. So once you settle, you settle.

Once you have recovered as much as possible, call the insurance company adjuster and tell them you are ready to settle. Tell the adjuster you will mail/fax them your diary and receipts. Send the information via 2-3 day Priority Mail with delivery confirmation. The adjuster will contact your workplace if you have lost wages. Once he has all the information he will make you an offer. The average time to settle your claim is approximately 30 days. For my medium accident it took 2 weeks. For my minor accident it took one day. I faxed the information, they contacted me with an initial offer, I said it wasn't enough and they gave me the second offer which I took.

Don't let your insurance adjuster sit on your claim but DO NOT KEEP phoning your adjuster. If you are too anxious they will try to settle with a low offer. It is doubtful that they will string a case out for a long time since they are measured in some companies for how fast they can close cases without going to court. If you counter offer from the initial offer and they say they need to check with their supervisor, get a specific date and time when they will call you back. If they don't get back call them and ask why.

Most offers are done over the phone but you may be called into their office for a face to face meeting. Similar to car salesman, you may feel more pressured to take the first offer but again if you have your figures in mind from the formula, stick to them. Don't be afraid to argue if you think it is too low, the first offer ALWAYS is. Adjusters are measured by how much they save the company in money.

Once the adjuster tells you that amount is as high as they can go or that is the final amount they are willing to offer, tell them you will think it over and get back to them. If it falls in your range and you are happy with the amount call the adjuster the next day and accept the offer. If the offer still is too low there is another avenue you can try. The Alternative Dispute Resolution (ADR) provides other options for settling injury claims. ADR works through mediation between you and the insurance company to determine a fair settlement. This is where the diary pays off! ADR takes your settlement over the adjusters head to a panel of judges.

Like court, insurance companies do not want to go through ADR so most likely they will increase the settlement if you mention ADR or that you may need to get a lawyer. The department of labor has a website that explains ADR and what is available in your area.

http://www.dol.gov/dol/asp/public/programs/adr/main.htm

If the settlement amount is fair, the insurance company will cut you a check and have you sign a release form. And you are done!

Chapter

11

Summary

Quick review

H ere is a summary of the topics discussed in this book. The summary can be used as a guideline for the tasks during each time period of before and after an accident.

BEFORE AN ACCIDENT

1) Review your insurance policy and coverage's with your insurance agent.

2) Keep a copy of the checklist which shows what to do at the scene of an accident in your glove compartment.

3) Buy a disposable camera and keep in your glove compartment.

AT AN ACCIDENT SCENE

1) Check everyone for serious injury - call police if needed.

2) Look for witnesses.

3) Protect the area - put flares out, put on your hazard lights etc.

4) Take pictures of the scene and surroundings.

5) Do not argue with the other driver but speak up when the police arrive.

6) Get information, exchange insurance cards/licenses/plate numbers - if your car needs towing, make sure you get the name and phone from the tow truck driver.

7) Do not sign anything.

8) Do not accept any form of payment from the other driver.

AFTER AN ACCIDENT

1) Relax and let the adrenaline wear off.

2) Write down your version of the accident even if you have given a police report.

3) Seek medical attention if needed and tell the doctors you were involved in a car accident.

4) File a police accident report if the police did not come to the scene. If the accident is minor you may not need to.

5) Phone your insurance company to report the accident.

6) Phone the other drivers company to open a claim.

7) Get a copy of the accident report.

8) Get a rental car if needed and speak with the garage about how long it will take to fix your car and the approximate cost.

9) Speak with a lawyer if you feel you would like an opinion on your minor/medium accident. GET a lawyer if you have been involved in a major serious accident.

10) Purchase any over the counter medicine, heating pads, etc that you need for your injuries and save all receipts. Your doctor may have suggestions for items outside of prescriptions.

11) Start your diary

12) Wait for your injuries to fully heal or heal as much as possible. If you need to see the doctor multiple times because of pain not healing do so.

13) When you have recovered fully, get all your expenses and apply the formula with various multipliers.

14) Call the adjuster to settle

15) When a fair offer has been presented, accept and cash the check.

Real Examples

Actual Examples from Real Life

H ere are some real world examples of actual accidents describing what happened step by step. This should help you understand the process (even though it varies between insurance companies and states)

Minor Accident

This accident happened on the way to work. I had traveled this same route every morning. This day, however, I was stopped at a 4 way intersection traffic light and waiting for it to change to green. I left plenty of space between the car in front of me (which you should always do at a stop light in case you are rear-ended). I had been stopped for about 30 seconds when another car from behind me from behind.

It was totally unexpected and I got out of my car to see what damage had been done. I have a hitch behind my SUV with an extension. It was a good thing I had that hitch extension on otherwise my rear bumper would have been substantial damaged. The other driver's car was still on my hitch extension! I first made sure no one was hurt and then I asked politely for them to back up off my car. The other driver was very cooperative, they didn't even get out of the car to inspect anything. The other driver asked if I would like to pull off the road at the next street (since we were at a busy intersection) to exchange information. Since it was a small accident the need for police and witnesses wasn't a major concern. Plus the damage was minor.

We exchanged information at the next street over. I took the other drivers insurance card and wrote down everything on it which including the VIN, address information and asked for their work and home phone number.

I did make one mistake however, since I knew what the hitch extension cost me I offered to not go against the other driver's insurance policy if they wanted to just pay me for the part. The other driver agreed. Once I got to work I started my diary.

I got home from work that day and called the other driver with the amount. I left a message on the answering machine to call me back and let me know. The next day came and went and no reply. I left one final message telling the other driver that if I didn't hear from them by 9:00pm I was going to file a claim with their insurance company. 9:00pm came and went with no call. Mistake #1 Trying to be nice. I was a little upset at first but then I thought that if I was in their position I would rather let my insurance company handle it too.

So at 9:00pm I called my insurance company to report the accident (for reference only), letting my company know that I would be filing a claim against the other drivers insurance policy. Next I called the other drivers insurance company to report the claim. They took all the information, assigned me a claim number and an insurance representative name/number that would be calling me the next day.

The next day, as promised, the other driver's insurance company called to setup an appraisal appointment to fix my car. At first they wanted me to drive to one of their centers (You don't have to do this), I felt that was inconvenient and they said they would send an adjuster to my place of work (the time range was 1 week and the adjuster would call me prior to coming out). They also asked how I was feeling. I told them my neck had some pain and my back hurt a little. I told them I was keeping a diary that I would like to try and settle the claim without a lawyer.

A week went by and the adjuster had not called to make an appointment. I called the other drivers insurance company and they apologized and setup an appointment for the next day. The next day the adjuster came to my office to review the damage. I had prepared by getting several quotes for the hitch extension. He took several pictures of the damaged area and reviewed my quote. He gave me a check on the spot for the part and labor to install it (since I was installing it the labor charge went to me). Two days later after the adjuster submitted the paperwork I was called by the other drivers insurance company and since I had labor on the adjusters paperwork, they also sent me another check for loss of use of my car (similar to renting a car).

Now the final piece was the medical. I had gone to the doctors the first week when my neck and back hurt. My doctor said it was soft tissue damage and said if by the second week I was not feeling better that I would need x-ray's. But by the second week I was feeling better so I decided to settle the medical.

I called the insurance company representative and was given another name/number of the person that would handle my medical claim (usually you will have 2 different representatives handling your claim, one for medical and one for auto damage). I told him I had some paperwork to fax to him. He asked me what that was. I told him it was receipts and a diary. He gave me a fax number and I faxed over the diary which included time missed from work. I also had calculated using the formula my low/medium and high range dollars that I would settle for.

Now that he had all the paperwork I waited for a call from him. You don't want to look too anxious so let them call you first. He called with a really low offer to settle. I told him that it was too low. He came back with the damage on the vehicle was small. I told him the damage of the vehicle has nothing to do with medical (which it doesn't, he knows that, he is just trying to settle for as little as possible). He asked me how much I was looking for and I would not give him a figure, I just told him to call me back after he reviews his numbers again.

He called back the next day with another figure which I told him was still too low. After I said that he came back with a number that was way over my high figure. He went too high too fast, his mistake. I took that figure and I received a check in 3 days.

If I had let the other driver just pay me for the part I would have never been reimbursed for my neck/back pain that I had for the 2 weeks. So remember, always follow the recommendations of this book.

Here is an actual diary entries from the minor accident the first day:

6/14

Used Flexall muscle relaxer on neck before bed   9:00pm
constant neck and back pain

Woke up with stabbing pain in neck area   3:00am
Took 2 advil

       Missed Recreation: not able to jetski
       Emotional: interference to sexual relations

✓ ALWAYS get the other drivers information, even if you don't see any damage. You may notice scratches, scrapes long after you let the other driver go. Also you never know how much of an injury that you or your passengers may have since most of the effects from an accident occur long after the accident.

✓ Don't be a nice guy because you never know what might be hiding from an accident (hidden damage, hidden physical injury). Remember you are going after the insurance company not the other driver.

✓ You have paid your insurance every year probably since you were sixteen. You have paid thousands of dollars to the insurance company over the years. When someone has an accident with you, you deserve to get some of your money back.

Medium Accident

This accident happened on a shopping trip on the weekend. I was stopped at a stop sign and had a passenger with me. It was sunny out with excellent driving conditions. It was a T intersection. I was looking to my right to check for traffic. All of a sudden my passenger screamed, a loud bang occurred and we both we jolted forward. I looked forward (since my head was turned looking for traffic) and an elderly lady had hit me head on! I still had my foot on the brake since I was at a stop sign. I made sure my passenger was ok, checked myself and then got out of the car to check on the other driver. She stated several times that it was all her fault and that she didn't see us.

There were no witnesses but a homeowner heard the accident and phoned the police. Everyone was ok. I left my car exactly where it was but the other driver moved her car so traffic could get by. We let the elderly woman use <u>our</u> cell phone to call her husband. We were being nice. The officer came to take the accident report since there was a lot of damage. He took my story of the accident then hers. I later found out from the accident report that she tried to blame me!! The officer however upon seeing my car damage believed my story. See what you get for being nice..nothing. Here we both were helping the elderly lady and in the end she tried to put us at fault saying we had pulled out in front of her.(If that was true I would have had damage on the side of my car not head on damage). Then when the officer told her based on the damage that it was her fault, she tried to blame the homeowner (who was nice and phoned police) saying that it was their hedges being too high that caused her to make an illegal left turn and hit me. Nice elderly lady huh!

I was able to drive my car home without being towed but it was seriously damaged. (If you need a tow make sure the driver goes to the auto body shop you want, don't let him talk you into bringing it to his or one that he recommends. You are entitled to go where you want.) The windshield was cracked, the hood crumpled, the radiator damaged and bumper was totally destroyed.

We got home and the first thing I did was call my insurance company to report the accident and let my company know that I was going after hers. The next thing was to call her company and get a claim number and then call a car rental agency to get a rental car. We went down and picked up a car (similar in value to what I drove) and gave the rental car company the other driver's insurance company and claim number. Next I called my dealer and asked where the auto body shop was for the dealership. They gave me the address and I drove my car to the auto body shop. I told the auto body shop to use only factory authorized parts for ALL the repairs including the windshield. I also asked how long it would take to complete the work (2 weeks), I then notified the car rental company.

So the car and my transportation was taken care of and I didn't outlay one penny. Next up was the pain we were both in. I started my diary and so did my passenger. We both had gone to work on Monday and we both hurt a lot and we were not sleeping. I called my passenger and asked if she wanted to get her injuries checked and get an x-ray. She did, so we both met after work and went to a walk in medical injury center that dealt with sport injuries. We both had to pay the initial cost for the visit and x-ray upfront. The doctor xray'd both of us and also gave us a prescription to fill along with over the counter drug recommendations. She also recommended physical therapy if we were still in a lot of pain The next stop was the drug store where we filled our prescriptions and purchased the over the counter drugs and lotions. We saved all the receipts from that day in a separate envelope that we kept with the diary.

I also had to call for a copy of the accident report, the other drivers insurance company wanted to make sure that the accident was 100% her fault. So I contacted the police department of the town the accident occurred in. It wasn't ready yet. I kept calling and it took the officer a week before it was finished. I guess this is typical of most departments so don't worry if it takes them awhile. However to get the report I had to go down to the station and pay 10$. Make sure you get a receipt and keep it with your diary, you will be reimbursed for all your expenses. I then faxed it to the insurance representative. He reviewed the report and agreed she was 100% at fault.

During the next several weeks I kept the diary up to date. The auto body shop called me in the second week to tell me that there was further damage to the car which they didn't see initially and that the adjuster would be coming out to inspect. The adjuster also tried to argue with me that the windshield crack was not caused by the accident but in the end told me he would replace it. He tried to tell me I always had a crack in it, which wasn't true. He also wasn't going to replace the hood since it only crumpled a little. He wanted the shop the bang it out and patch it. I told him that my car needs to be put back to its original state before the accident, which didn't include patches. He told me he would ok a new hood.

It was going to take an extra week though for the hidden damage so I called the insurance company to notify them and then the rental car company to extend my rental. I was still on a lot of pain medication and so was my passenger. We both were experiencing a lot of pain still in the third week. My car was ready in the fourth week, so I returned the rental car and picked up my car at the auto body shop. The dealership did a great job on the car and I accepted the work by signing the invoice. I didn't have to pay anything since the insurance company had sent the check to the auto body shop for the damage, and the car rental company billed the insurance company for the final balance.

By the fourth week we both still were not back to normal health with our neck and back injury so we decided to wait to file the medical claim portion of the accident. The insurance company would call now and then to check on how we were doing. When the company does this, DO NOT tell them you are feeling better at any point. An injury can change quickly so you should not give any specifics and just tell them you will contact them when you are feeling better.

Around the 8th week we both were feeling better, the muscles in our necks and backs were healing and the muscle tissue had improved greatly. So we gathered all of our receipts and both diaries and called the other drivers insurance company and told them we were ready

TO TRY and settle without a lawyer. By stating it that way it tells the insurance company that if they don't try to reasonably settle, then you will get a lawyer.

This information was too large to fax so I mailed it via Priority Mail with delivery tracking. Delivery tracking allows you to have a record of the mailing. I used the formula to come up with 3 ranges (High/Medium/Low) for each of us (my passenger and myself). The insurance company called 3 days after receiving the information and gave me a low figure first (they usually do). I told him I thought the amount was too low. He asked what I had in mind, I told him to reconsider everything in the diaries and come up with another figure. He called back the next day with a figure that was in between the medium and high figure which I thought was fair. He also gave my passenger the same range amount. So I told him I would check with my passenger to see if she agreed.

I called him the next day and said I would agree to the 2 amounts. Within 2 days we both were sent separate checks and the claim settlement was complete.

- ✓ **Follow up with the accident report since this shows proof of who was at fault. If it was written up incorrectly discuss the situation with the officer and bring your photos if you have them.**

- ✓ **Again, Do not be nice! That doesn't mean you have to be mean just be polite but state your case. Remember you are going after the insurance company not the other driver.**

- ✓ **Wait till your injuries have completely healed before you settle on your injury.**

Here are some actual diary entries from the medium accident:

7/13

2 advil take 2 hours after accident   6:00pm
constant neck and back pain

2 advil before bed   10:00pm

Special Event : missed Lucy's 40th birthday
Emotional: interference to sexual relations

7/14

woke up at 2:30am neck/back pain couldn't sleep 2:30 am
till 3:30am took 2 advil

woke up 9:00am took 2 advil for neck/back pain   9:00am

Missed Recreation: not able to jetski
Emotional: interference to sexual relations

advil throughout the day for neck and back pain

7/15

woke up 4:30 am with back pain   4:30am
took 2 advils

took 2 advils before work, back pain   6:30am

left work early due to back pain   12:30pm   **1.5 hours**
of work

missed + 1 hour
overtime

Forms

The first 2 forms following this page should be kept in the glove compartment of your car along with a disposable camera and a pen. The first sheet is an accident sheet which you should use to gather all the information from the scene, the second sheet is to record any witness and passenger information.

You should be able to fill in most of the information on the sheets but don't worry if it is not complete. Just try to get as much information as you can, no matter how small the accident is.

On the third and fourth pages following this one is a sample diary. You should fill this out as thoroughly as possible. In the beginning you should make entries every day even every hour during the day and night as you feel pain and discomfort. Then as time goes on and you are healing, the entries should still be done every day but may not contain hourly entries.

1.

- [✓] 1. Check Everyone
- [✓] 2. Look for Witnesses
- [✓] 3. Protect the Area
- [✓] 4. Take Pictures
- [✓] 5. Speak Up
- [✓] 6. Get Info Below
- [✓] 7. Don't Sign Anything
- [✓] 8. Don't Accept Payment

Accident Information

Date: _____ Time: _____ AM: ___ PM: ___

Street/Highway: _____

Intersection: _____

City: _____ State: _____ Zip Code: _____

Police Name: _____ Case #: _____

Ticket issued (Y/N) _____ To who: _____ Type Ticket: _____

Other Car Insurance Card / License Information

Driver Name: _____ Registered Owner: _____

Address: _____ Address: _____

City: _____ State: _____ Zip Code: _____

Drivers License #: _____ State: _____ License Plate: _____

Car Make: _____ Model: _____ Color: _____

Insurance Co: _____ Policy #: _____

Fill In Diagram with Cars, Position of Accident, Note Direction with Arrows, Traffic Lights/Signs

2.

 1. Check Everyone   3. Protect the Area   6. Get Info Below

✓ 2. Look for Witnesses   ✓ 4. Take Pictures   ✓ 7. Don't Sign Anything

✓ 5. Speak Up   ✓ 8. Don't Accept Payment

Witness Information

Name: _____   Phone: _____

Address: _____

City: _____   State: _____   Zip Code: _____

Name: _____   Phone: _____

Address: _____

City: _____   State: _____   Zip Code: _____

Name: _____   Phone: _____

Address: _____

City: _____   State: _____   Zip Code: _____

Passengers Information

Other Driver:

Name: _____   Apparent Injuries (Y/N): _____

Address: _____

City: _____   State: _____   Zip Code: _____

Name: _____   Apparent Injuries (Y/N): _____

Address: _____

City: _____   State: _____   Zip Code: _____

Name: _____   Apparent Injuries (Y/N): _____

Address: _____

City: _____   State: _____   Zip Code: _____

YOURS:

Name: _____   Apparent Injuries (Y/N): _____

Address: _____

City: _____   State: _____   Zip Code: _____

Name: _____   Apparent Injuries (Y/N): _____

Address: _____

City: _____   State: _____   Zip Code: _____

Name: _____   Apparent Injuries (Y/N): _____

Address: _____

City: _____   State: _____   Zip Code: _____

1.

☑ 1. Check Everyone ☑ 3. Protect the Area ☑ 6. Get Info Below

☑ 2. Look for Witnesses ☑ 4. Take Pictures ☑ 7. Don't Sign Anything

☑ 5. Speak Up ☑ 8. Don't Accept Payment

Accident Information

Date: _____ Time: _____ AM: ___ PM: ___

Street/Highway: _____

Intersection: _____

City: _____ State: _____ Zip Code: _____

Police Name: _____ Case #: _____

Ticket issued (Y/N) _____ To who: _____ Type Ticket: _____

Other Car Insurance Card / License Information

Driver Name: _____ Registered Owner: _____

Address: _____ Address: _____

City: _____ State: _____ Zip Code: _____

Drivers License #: _____ State: _____ License Plate: _____

Car Make: _____ Model: _____ Color: _____

Insurance Co: _____ Policy #: _____

Fill In Diagram with Cars, Position of Accident, Note Direction with Arrows, Traffic Lights/Signs

2.

 1. Check Everyone   3. Protect the Area   6. Get Info Below

☑ 2. Look for Witnesses   ☑ 4. Take Pictures   ☑ 7. Don't Sign Anything

☑ 5. Speak Up   ☑ 8. Don't Accept Payment

Witness Information

Name: _____ Phone: _____

Address: _____

City: _____ State: _____ Zip Code: _____

Name: _____ Phone: _____

Address: _____

City: _____ State: _____ Zip Code: _____

Name: _____ Phone: _____

Address: _____

City: _____ State: _____ Zip Code: _____

Passengers Information

Other Driver:

Name: _____ Apparent Injuries (Y/N): _____

Address: _____

City: _____ State: _____ Zip Code: _____

Name: _____ Apparent Injuries (Y/N): _____

Address: _____

City: _____ State: _____ Zip Code: _____

Name: _____ Apparent Injuries (Y/N): _____

Address: _____

City: _____ State: _____ Zip Code: _____

YOURS:

Name: _____ Apparent Injuries (Y/N): _____

Address: _____

City: _____ State: _____ Zip Code: _____

Name: _____ Apparent Injuries (Y/N): _____

Address: _____

City: _____ State: _____ Zip Code: _____

Name: _____ Apparent Injuries (Y/N): _____

Address: _____

City: _____ State: _____ Zip Code: _____

1.

☑ 1. Check Everyone ☑ 3. Protect the Area ☑ 6. Get Info Below

☑ 2. Look for Witnesses ☑ 4. Take Pictures ☑ 7. Don't Sign Anything

☑ 5. Speak Up ☑ 8. Don't Accept Payment

Accident Information

Date: _____ Time: _____ AM: ___ PM: ___

Street/Highway: _____

Intersection: _____

City: _____ State: _____ Zip Code: _____

Police Name: _____ Case #: _____

Ticket issued (Y/N) _____ To who: _____ Type Ticket: _____

Other Car Insurance Card / License Information

Driver Name: _____ Registered Owner: _____

Address: _____ Address: _____

City: _____ State: _____ Zip Code: _____

Drivers License #: _____ State: _____ License Plate: _____

Car Make: _____ Model: _____ Color: _____

Insurance Co: _____ Policy #: _____

Fill In Diagram with Cars, Position of Accident, Note Direction with Arrows, Traffic Lights/Signs

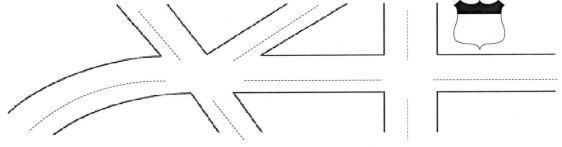

2.

1. Check Everyone   3. Protect the Area   6. Get Info Below

2. Look for Witnesses   4. Take Pictures   7. Don't Sign Anything

5. Speak Up   8. Don't Accept Payment

Witness Information

Name: _____   Phone: _____

Address: _____

City: _____   State: _____   Zip Code: _____

Name: _____   Phone: _____

Address: _____

City: _____   State: _____   Zip Code: _____

Name: _____   Phone: _____

Address: _____

City: _____   State: _____   Zip Code: _____

Passengers Information

Other Driver:

Name: _____   Apparent Injuries (Y/N): _____

Address: _____

City: _____   State: _____   Zip Code: _____

Name: _____   Apparent Injuries (Y/N): _____

Address: _____

City: _____   State: _____   Zip Code: _____

Name: _____   Apparent Injuries (Y/N): _____

Address: _____

City: _____   State: _____   Zip Code: _____

YOURS:

Name: _____   Apparent Injuries (Y/N): _____

Address: _____

City: _____   State: _____   Zip Code: _____

Name: _____   Apparent Injuries (Y/N): _____

Address: _____

City: _____   State: _____   Zip Code: _____

Name: _____   Apparent Injuries (Y/N): _____

Address: _____

City: _____   State: _____   Zip Code: _____

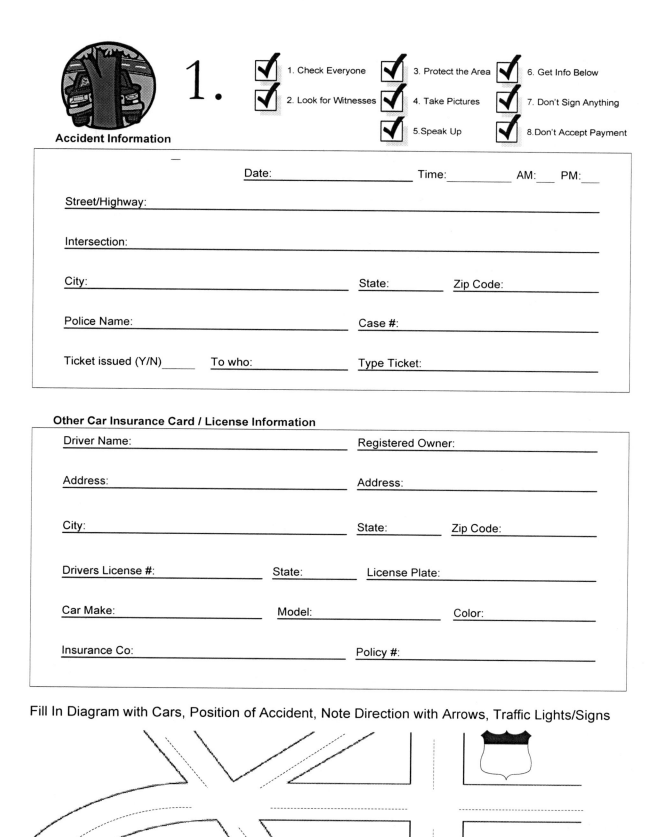

1.

☑ 1. Check Everyone   ☑ 3. Protect the Area   ☑ 6. Get Info Below

☑ 2. Look for Witnesses   ☑ 4. Take Pictures   ☑ 7. Don't Sign Anything

☑ 5.Speak Up   ☑ 8.Don't Accept Payment

Accident Information

Date: _____ Time: _____ AM: ___ PM: ___

Street/Highway: _____

Intersection: _____

City: _____ State: _____ Zip Code: _____

Police Name: _____ Case #: _____

Ticket issued (Y/N) _____ To who: _____ Type Ticket: _____

Other Car Insurance Card / License Information

Driver Name: _____ Registered Owner: _____

Address: _____ Address: _____

City: _____ State: _____ Zip Code: _____

Drivers License #: _____ State: _____ License Plate: _____

Car Make: _____ Model: _____ Color: _____

Insurance Co: _____ Policy #: _____

Fill In Diagram with Cars, Position of Accident, Note Direction with Arrows, Traffic Lights/Signs

2.

☑ 1. Check Everyone ☑ 3. Protect the Area ☑ 6. Get Info Below

☑ 2. Look for Witnesses ☑ 4. Take Pictures ☑ 7. Don't Sign Anything

☑ 5. Speak Up ☑ 8. Don't Accept Payment

Witness Information

Name: _____ Phone: _____

Address: _____

City: _____ State: _____ Zip Code: _____

Name: _____ Phone: _____

Address: _____

City: _____ State: _____ Zip Code: _____

Name: _____ Phone: _____

Address: _____

City: _____ State: _____ Zip Code: _____

Passengers Information

Other Driver:

Name: _____ Apparent Injuries (Y/N): _____

Address: _____

City: _____ State: _____ Zip Code: _____

Name: _____ Apparent Injuries (Y/N): _____

Address: _____

City: _____ State: _____ Zip Code: _____

Name: _____ Apparent Injuries (Y/N): _____

Address: _____

City: _____ State: _____ Zip Code: _____

YOURS:

Name: _____ Apparent Injuries (Y/N): _____

Address: _____

City: _____ State: _____ Zip Code: _____

Name: _____ Apparent Injuries (Y/N): _____

Address: _____

City: _____ State: _____ Zip Code: _____

Name: _____ Apparent Injuries (Y/N): _____

Address: _____

City: _____ State: _____ Zip Code: _____

1.

☑ 1. Check Everyone ☑ 3. Protect the Area ☑ 6. Get Info Below

☑ 2. Look for Witnesses ☑ 4. Take Pictures ☑ 7. Don't Sign Anything

☑ 5. Speak Up ☑ 8. Don't Accept Payment

Accident Information

Date: _____ Time: _____ AM: ___ PM: ___

Street/Highway: _____

Intersection: _____

City: _____ State: _____ Zip Code: _____

Police Name: _____ Case #: _____

Ticket issued (Y/N) _____ To who: _____ Type Ticket: _____

Other Car Insurance Card / License Information

Driver Name: _____ Registered Owner: _____

Address: _____ Address: _____

City: _____ State: _____ Zip Code: _____

Drivers License #: _____ State: _____ License Plate: _____

Car Make: _____ Model: _____ Color: _____

Insurance Co: _____ Policy #: _____

Fill In Diagram with Cars, Position of Accident, Note Direction with Arrows, Traffic Lights/Signs

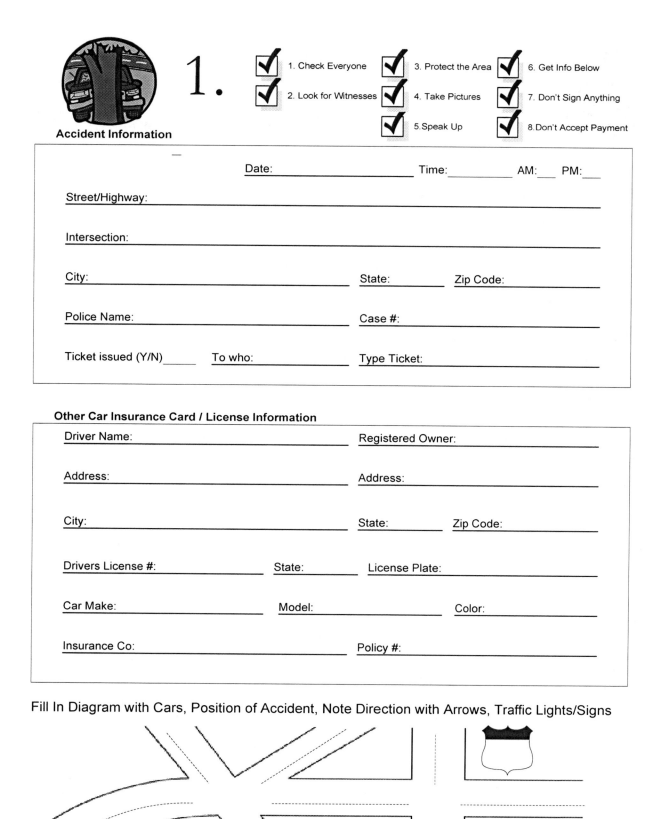

2.

1. Check Everyone   3. Protect the Area   6. Get Info Below

2. Look for Witnesses   4. Take Pictures   7. Don't Sign Anything

5. Speak Up   8. Don't Accept Payment

Witness Information

Name: _____   Phone: _____

Address: _____

City: _____   State: _____   Zip Code: _____

Name: _____   Phone: _____

Address: _____

City: _____   State: _____   Zip Code: _____

Name: _____   Phone: _____

Address: _____

City: _____   State: _____   Zip Code: _____

Passengers Information

Other Driver:

Name: _____   Apparent Injuries (Y/N): _____

Address: _____

City: _____   State: _____   Zip Code: _____

Name: _____   Apparent Injuries (Y/N): _____

Address: _____

City: _____   State: _____   Zip Code: _____

Name: _____   Apparent Injuries (Y/N): _____

Address: _____

City: _____   State: _____   Zip Code: _____

YOURS:

Name: _____   Apparent Injuries (Y/N): _____

Address: _____

City: _____   State: _____   Zip Code: _____

Name: _____   Apparent Injuries (Y/N): _____

Address: _____

City: _____   State: _____   Zip Code: _____

Name: _____   Apparent Injuries (Y/N): _____

Address: _____

City: _____   State: _____   Zip Code: _____

DIARY

Your Insurance Company: _____ Phone: _____

Name Adjuster you reported to: _____

Claim # assigned: _____

Other Drivers Insurance Company: _____ Phone: _____

Name Adjuster you reported to: _____

Claim # assigned: _____

Auto Body Name: _____ Phone: _____

Repairman name: _____

Tow truck company: _____ Phone: _____

Short Description of Accident: _____

_____

_____

_____

_____

Date: _____ Time: _____ AM: ___ PM: ___

Description of Pain/Injury: _____

_____

_____

_____

Medication Taken: _____   Medication Expense: _____

Doctor/Hospital Location/ Type Visit: _____   Doctor/Hospital Expense: _____

Missed Recreational/Emotional: _____   Missed hours of work: _____

Date: _____ Time: _____ AM: ___ PM: ___

Description of Pain/Injury: _____

_____

_____

_____

Medication Taken: _____   Medication Expense: _____

Doctor/Hospital Location/ Type Visit: _____   Doctor/Hospital Expense: _____

Missed Recreational/Emotional: _____   Missed hours of work: _____

DIARY

Your Insurance Company: _____ Phone: _____

Name Adjuster you reported to: _____

Claim # assigned: _____

Other Drivers Insurance Company: _____ Phone: _____

Name Adjuster you reported to: _____

Claim # assigned: _____

Auto Body Name: _____ Phone: _____

Repairman name: _____

Tow truck company: _____ Phone: _____

Short Description of Accident: _____

_____

_____

_____

_____

Date: _____ Time: _____ AM:___ PM:___

Description of Pain/Injury: _____

_____

_____

_____

Medication Taken: _____ Medication Expense: _____

Doctor/Hospital Location/ Type Visit: _____ Doctor/Hospital Expense: _____

Missed Recreational/Emotional: _____ Missed hours of work: _____

Date: _____ Time: _____ AM:___ PM:___

Description of Pain/Injury: _____

_____

_____

_____

Medication Taken: _____ Medication Expense: _____

Doctor/Hospital Location/ Type Visit: _____ Doctor/Hospital Expense: _____

Missed Recreational/Emotional: _____ Missed hours of work: _____

DIARY

Your Insurance Company: _____   Phone: _____

Name Adjuster you reported to: _____

Claim # assigned: _____

Other Drivers Insurance Company: _____   Phone: _____

Name Adjuster you reported to: _____

Claim # assigned: _____

Auto Body Name: _____   Phone: _____

Repairman name: _____

Tow truck company: _____   Phone: _____

Short Description of Accident: _____

_____

_____

_____

Date: _____   Time: _____   AM: ____   PM: ____

Description of Pain/Injury: _____

_____

_____

_____

Medication Taken: _____   Medication Expense: _____

Doctor/Hospital Location/ Type Visit: _____   Doctor/Hospital Expense: _____

Missed Recreational/Emotional: _____   Missed hours of work: _____

Date: _____   Time: _____   AM: ____   PM: ____

Description of Pain/Injury: _____

_____

_____

_____

Medication Taken: _____   Medication Expense: _____

Doctor/Hospital Location/ Type Visit: _____   Doctor/Hospital Expense: _____

Missed Recreational/Emotional: _____   Missed hours of work: _____

DIARY

Your Insurance Company: _____ Phone: _____

Name Adjuster you reported to: _____

Claim # assigned: _____

Other Drivers Insurance Company: _____ Phone: _____

Name Adjuster you reported to: _____

Claim # assigned: _____

Auto Body Name: _____ Phone: _____

Repairman name: _____

Tow truck company: _____ Phone: _____

Short Description of Accident: _____

_____

_____

_____

Date: _____ Time: _____ AM: ___ PM: ___

Description of Pain/Injury: _____

_____

_____

_____

Medication Taken: _____   Medication Expense: _____

Doctor/Hospital Location/ Type Visit: _____   Doctor/Hospital Expense: _____

Missed Recreational/Emotional: _____   Missed hours of work: _____

Date: _____ Time: _____ AM: ___ PM: ___

Description of Pain/Injury: _____

_____

_____

_____

Medication Taken: _____   Medication Expense: _____

Doctor/Hospital Location/ Type Visit: _____   Doctor/Hospital Expense: _____

Missed Recreational/Emotional: _____   Missed hours of work: _____

DIARY

Your Insurance Company: _____   Phone: _____

Name Adjuster you reported to: _____

Claim # assigned: _____

Other Drivers Insurance Company: _____   Phone: _____

Name Adjuster you reported to: _____

Claim # assigned: _____

Auto Body Name: _____   Phone: _____

Repairman name: _____

Tow truck company: _____   Phone: _____

Short Description of Accident: _____
_____
_____
_____
_____

Date: _____   Time: _____   AM: ___   PM: ___

Description of Pain/Injury: _____
_____
_____
_____

Medication Taken: _____   Medication Expense: _____

Doctor/Hospital Location/ Type Visit: _____   Doctor/Hospital Expense: _____

Missed Recreational/Emotional: _____   Missed hours of work: _____

Date: _____   Time: _____   AM: ___   PM: ___

Description of Pain/Injury: _____
_____
_____
_____

Medication Taken: _____   Medication Expense: _____

Doctor/Hospital Location/ Type Visit: _____   Doctor/Hospital Expense: _____

Missed Recreational/Emotional: _____   Missed hours of work: _____

DIARY

Your Insurance Company: _____ Phone: _____

Name Adjuster you reported to: _____

Claim # assigned: _____

Other Drivers Insurance Company: _____ Phone: _____

Name Adjuster you reported to: _____

Claim # assigned: _____

Auto Body Name: _____ Phone: _____

Repairman name: _____

Tow truck company: _____ Phone: _____

Short Description of Accident: _____
_____
_____
_____
_____

Date: _____ Time: _____ AM: ___ PM: ___

Description of Pain/Injury: _____
_____
_____
_____

Medication Taken: _____ Medication Expense: _____

Doctor/Hospital Location/ Type Visit: _____ Doctor/Hospital Expense: _____

Missed Recreational/Emotional: _____ Missed hours of work: _____

Date: _____ Time: _____ AM: ___ PM: ___

Description of Pain/Injury: _____
_____
_____

Medication Taken: _____ Medication Expense: _____

Doctor/Hospital Location/ Type Visit: _____ Doctor/Hospital Expense: _____

Missed Recreational/Emotional: _____ Missed hours of work: _____

DIARY

Your Insurance Company: _____ Phone: _____

Name Adjuster you reported to: _____

Claim # assigned: _____

Other Drivers Insurance Company: _____ Phone: _____

Name Adjuster you reported to: _____

Claim # assigned: _____

Auto Body Name: _____ Phone: _____

Repairman name: _____

Tow truck company: _____ Phone: _____

Short Description of Accident: _____

_____

_____

_____

Date: _____ Time: _____ AM: ___ PM: ___

Description of Pain/Injury: _____

_____

_____

_____

Medication Taken: _____ Medication Expense: _____

Doctor/Hospital Location/ Type Visit: _____ Doctor/Hospital Expense: _____

Missed Recreational/Emotional: _____ Missed hours of work: _____

Date: _____ Time: _____ AM: ___ PM: ___

Description of Pain/Injury: _____

_____

_____

Medication Taken: _____ Medication Expense: _____

Doctor/Hospital Location/ Type Visit: _____ Doctor/Hospital Expense: _____

Missed Recreational/Emotional: _____ Missed hours of work: _____

DIARY

Your Insurance Company: _____ Phone: _____

Name Adjuster you reported to: _____

Claim # assigned: _____

Other Drivers Insurance Company: _____ Phone: _____

Name Adjuster you reported to: _____

Claim # assigned: _____

Auto Body Name: _____ Phone: _____

Repairman name: _____

Tow truck company: _____ Phone: _____

Short Description of Accident: _____

_____

_____

_____

_____

Date: _____ Time: _____ AM: ___ PM: ___

Description of Pain/Injury: _____

_____

_____

_____

Medication Taken: _____   Medication Expense: _____

Doctor/Hospital Location/ Type Visit: _____   Doctor/Hospital Expense: _____

Missed Recreational/Emotional: _____   Missed hours of work: _____

Date: _____ Time: _____ AM: ___ PM: ___

Description of Pain/Injury: _____

_____

_____

_____

Medication Taken: _____   Medication Expense: _____

Doctor/Hospital Location/ Type Visit: _____   Doctor/Hospital Expense: _____

Missed Recreational/Emotional: _____   Missed hours of work: _____

DIARY

Your Insurance Company: _____ Phone: _____

Name Adjuster you reported to: _____

Claim # assigned: _____

Other Drivers Insurance Company: _____ Phone: _____

Name Adjuster you reported to: _____

Claim # assigned: _____

Auto Body Name: _____ Phone: _____

Repairman name: _____

Tow truck company: _____ Phone: _____

Short Description of Accident: _____

_____

_____

_____

Date: _____ Time: _____ AM: ___ PM: ___

Description of Pain/Injury: _____

_____

_____

_____

Medication Taken: _____ Medication Expense: _____

Doctor/Hospital Location/ Type Visit: _____ Doctor/Hospital Expense: _____

Missed Recreational/Emotional: _____ Missed hours of work: _____

Date: _____ Time: _____ AM: ___ PM: ___

Description of Pain/Injury: _____

_____

_____

_____

Medication Taken: _____ Medication Expense: _____

Doctor/Hospital Location/ Type Visit: _____ Doctor/Hospital Expense: _____

Missed Recreational/Emotional: _____ Missed hours of work: _____

DIARY

Your Insurance Company: _____   Phone: _____

Name Adjuster you reported to: _____

Claim # assigned: _____

Other Drivers Insurance Company: _____   Phone: _____

Name Adjuster you reported to: _____

Claim # assigned: _____

Auto Body Name: _____   Phone: _____

Repairman name: _____

Tow truck company: _____   Phone: _____

Short Description of Accident: _____

_____

_____

_____

Date: _____   Time: _____ AM: ___ PM: ___

Description of Pain/Injury: _____

_____

_____

_____

Medication Taken: _____   Medication Expense: _____

Doctor/Hospital Location/ Type Visit: _____   Doctor/Hospital Expense: _____

Missed Recreational/Emotional: _____   Missed hours of work: _____

Date: _____   Time: _____ AM: ___ PM: ___

Description of Pain/Injury: _____

_____

_____

_____

Medication Taken: _____   Medication Expense: _____

Doctor/Hospital Location/ Type Visit: _____   Doctor/Hospital Expense: _____

Missed Recreational/Emotional: _____   Missed hours of work: _____

DIARY

Your Insurance Company: _____   Phone: _____

Name Adjuster you reported to: _____

Claim # assigned: _____

Other Drivers Insurance Company: _____   Phone: _____

Name Adjuster you reported to: _____

Claim # assigned: _____

Auto Body Name: _____   Phone: _____

Repairman name: _____

Tow truck company: _____   Phone: _____

Short Description of Accident: _____

_____

_____

_____

Date: _____   Time: _____ AM:___ PM:___

Description of Pain/Injury: _____

_____

_____

Medication Taken: _____   Medication Expense: _____

Doctor/Hospital Location/ Type Visit: _____   Doctor/Hospital Expense: _____

Missed Recreational/Emotional: _____   Missed hours of work: _____

Date: _____   Time: _____ AM:___ PM:___

Description of Pain/Injury: _____

_____

_____

Medication Taken: _____   Medication Expense: _____

Doctor/Hospital Location/ Type Visit: _____   Doctor/Hospital Expense: _____

Missed Recreational/Emotional: _____   Missed hours of work: _____

Printed in the United States
102675LV00002B/161-162/A

9 781411 622135

This page left intentionally blank

Index

DIARY

Your Insurance Company: _____ Phone: _____

Name Adjuster you reported to: _____

Claim # assigned: _____

Other Drivers Insurance Company: _____ Phone: _____

Name Adjuster you reported to: _____

Claim # assigned: _____

Auto Body Name: _____ Phone: _____

Repairman name: _____

Tow truck company: _____ Phone: _____

Short Description of Accident: _____

_____

_____

_____

_____

Date: _____ Time: _____ AM: ___ PM: ___

Description of Pain/Injury: _____

_____

_____

_____

Medication Taken: _____   Medication Expense: _____

Doctor/Hospital Location/ Type Visit: _____   Doctor/Hospital Expense: _____

Missed Recreational/Emotional: _____   Missed hours of work: _____

Date: _____ Time: _____ AM: ___ PM: ___

Description of Pain/Injury: _____

_____

_____

_____

Medication Taken: _____   Medication Expense: _____

Doctor/Hospital Location/ Type Visit: _____   Doctor/Hospital Expense: _____

Missed Recreational/Emotional: _____   Missed hours of work: _____

This page left intentionally blank

Index

Printed in the United States
102675LV00002B/161-162/A